SILVER SERIES OF GROWN-UP WISDOM

EDITH EXCUSE

Janet Snyder and Kathleen Canova

Published by
Hasmark Publishing International
www.hasmarkpublishing.com

Copyright © 2024 Janet Snyder & Kathleen Canova

First Edition

No part of this book may be reproduced or transmitted in any form or by any means, electronic or mechanical, including photocopying, recording or by any information storage and retrieval system, without written permission from the author, except for the inclusion of brief quotations in a review.

Disclaimer:

This book is designed to provide information and motivation to our readers. It is sold with the understanding that the publisher is not engaged to render any type of psychological, legal, or any other kind of professional advice. The content of each article is the sole expression and opinion of its author, and not necessarily that of the publisher. No warranties or guarantees are expressed or implied by the publisher's choice to include any of the content in this volume. Neither the publisher nor the individual author(s) shall be liable for any physical, psychological, emotional, financial, or commercial damages, including, but not limited to, special, incidental, consequential or other damages. Our views and rights are the same: You are responsible for your own choices, actions, and results.

Permission should be addressed in writing to Janet & Kathy at janet@storybookpath.com

Cover Design: Anne Karklins [anne@hasmarkpublishing.com]
Interior Layout: Amit Dey [amit@hasmarkpublishing.com]
Illustrations: Chris Karrer

ISBN 13: 978-1-77482-302-6
ISBN 10: 1-77482-302-0

Dedication

We dedicate this book to all the "Ediths" in the world.

Additionally, we dedicate this book to the extremely talented artist and illustrator, Chris Karrer.

His architectural details, bold use of color, and bringing our fictional characters to life help us tell this great story about friendship.

From the bottom of our hearts, we thank you!

Acknowledgements

In gratitude for the unconditional love, encouragement, and support we've received from our **families** ~ those we were born into as well as those we helped create.

In gratitude for our dear **friends** who've been on this writing journey with us, especially those who have continued to coax and cheer us onward for years.

In gratitude for our brilliant **behind-the-scene creative duo**, Kimberly Lauersdorf and Kristan Clark, with candid critiques, enthusiastic readings, and challenging prep-talks.

In gratitude for the **crowd-funding** opportunity through BackerKit, and especially Lafia Morrow's leadership, laughter and navigation of this innovative financial pathway.

In gratitude for the **co-publishing** partnership with Hasmark Publishing International, especially its Founder, Judy O'Beirn's personal buy-in of this project and Jenn Gibson's capable leadership and coordination of their talented team.

In gratitude for the **lived experiences** we write about, because life is definitely not a spectator's sport; and we're proudly battle-tested warriors, now stronger, wiser and more compassionate having traveled these roads.

In gratitude for the **faith and freedom** to be true to ourselves, willing to tell bold stories, the good, the bad and the ugly; truly a legacy project for our culturally-relevant times.

In gratitude to **The Maker of Heaven and Earth, The Divine One** who introduced us to each other as teenagers, so that we could ultimately fulfill our life's purpose these many decades later, creating works of art and entertainment that will inspire humans forever.

In gratitude of our banner, **Silver Series of Grown-Up Wisdom**, a divine gift that we hold sacred, as we commit to creating and nurturing a genre of those "becoming" and "being" grown-up. It has been said, "it takes a village" to raise a child; and we believe that holds true when raising up "big kids" too. May our thought-provoking, illustrated short stories for grown-ups warm the hearts and minds of our beloved readers, and flourish for many generations.

It's part of human nature to make excuses, but has it become your last name? An excuse can free us from an obligation or duty. It can be an explanation offered to justify an action or make it better understood; however, *we can sometimes take it a bit too far!*

Edith seems to have more unresolved problems than her best friend from childhood, Ellie. Both were seven years old when they became neighbors and fast friends. They went to the same elementary school and on to the same high school together.

"E&E," as they've affectionately been called, were inseparable, until they turned eighteen and started taking an interest in men.

Edith was interested in the guys known as "Bad Boys!" You know, the cute ones with lots of somewhat childlike behavior. Maybe you've heard them called a man-child.

"They are the best kissers," Edith would swoon in gleeful explanation to Ellie, her very best friend. Ellie just chuckled at her dear friend, Edith.

Edith always seemed to do a dramatic *song and dance* when she needed an excuse not to participate in certain activities with Ellie. But, then again, she could be very evasive at other times.

Through the years, Edith has always done most of the talking while Ellie has always been an excellent listener. That continues on their phone calls these days.

It seems that once they had grown apart, while married and raising children, Ellie could see Edith's *excuse patterns* more clearly than ever before.

Knowing that her dear friend Edith would probably have a *cover story*, Ellie still decided to throw out an invitation for dinner.

"A bunch of us girls are getting together Friday and meeting at the Fish House for dinner," said Ellie. "Why don't you join us, Edith?"

"We have so much fun acting like silly schoolgirls and talking about things such as our *growing inability to hold in a fart!*"

"You should see my hair!" chuckled Edith with amusement. "It's out of control. So damn dry; I'm afraid it's going to break! I can't go out looking like this!"

"I use a great hair moisturizer that will work wonders for you too!" offered Ellie. But before Ellie could say the brand name, Edith replied, "Oh, I can't use anything like that. I have terrible allergies to all sorts of things."

Ellie then let Edith know the ingredients for this specific moisturizer were simply organic.

"I don't know nothin' about organic!" Edith chimed.

Sometimes they have silly conversations, joking about sitting there while talking on the phone together, without wearing a bra, and kibitzing about how far south their tatas have traveled.

"I'm sitting here at my kitchen table," said Ellie, "and I have my boobs slapped right on the tabletop for support. This is way more comfortable than that damn mammogram I had last week, squishing my tatas flat as a pancake!"

"Hey, I'm still not ruling out a good boobie lift, even at my age!"

They scream with rambunctious laughter!

Edith and Ellie were both widows in their seventies now, so their phone conversations had become more frequent, and Ellie was trying to make the best of it.

"Remember when we used to dance the night away at the community 'Teen Club,' Edith? It was so much fun and we absolutely loved the feel and the excitement of the music!"

"There's going to be a band in the square next weekend and the weather is supposed to be gorgeous. Let's dust off our outdoor folding chairs and take in some live music," suggested Ellie.

"I do remember that; we were just young chicks. It was so long ago and at least we were indoors. I haven't sat outside in years," quipped Edith. "The bugs just eat me alive."

"I hate any kind of bug and they hate me. Especially those damn mosquitos. No thank you!!"

"We can take some bug repellent," offered Ellie, but she was interrupted by Edith.

"I'm allergic to all that stuff, and don't start talking about organic shit again!"

"And I am not interested in all those healthy 'Health' foods either. They cost a FORTUNE!"

"On a good day, I can get a large order of fries from McDonald's for a dollar!"

Edith was always ready with a good *defense*.

"Are you still going to the gym and working out, Ellie?" asked Edith.

"Sure am, three days a week. Wanna join me one morning?"

"You can use a treadmill, elliptical, stationary bike and all kinds of strength and muscle-toning machines," answered Ellie, offering a feel-good activity that she believed was vital at this season of their lives.

"I don't know anything about those machines. Sounds like something that would make me sweat, and I hate sweating!!!"

Edith almost always answered without hesitation and *justification*. Then Edith would use her favorite *alibi*.

"Besides, my daughter, Evelyn, likes to stop by in the mornings."

"Well, Edith, walking is great exercise and doesn't make you sweat. It's easy peasy. You can walk at whatever time is best for you on any given day. All you need is a good pair of sneakers. Why don't you give it a go?!" quipped Ellie.

"What the hell, Ellie? I'm not stepping out and walking up and down these hills around here. Somebody will run my big ass over! Have you seen how much traffic is running through my neighborhood lately?! I know we have sidewalks but I'm scared to death to cross one of these busy streets."

Ellie, being a loving, kind-hearted friend, changed the subject and asked Edith, "What have you been doing since we talked last week?"

"Well, I had my primary care doctor visit the other day," replied Edith.

"Get this!" She screeched with disgust.

"My doctor said I need to lose weight! He is officially a *'Quack!'*"

"I knew it the first time I laid eyes on him. I'm kicking him to the curb and finding an intelligent, compassionate doctor. A doctor that knows, *big is beautiful!!*"

Ellie couldn't help but laugh with Edith, while shaking her head and rolling her eyes.

Edith chuckled at Ellie's suggestion, as she rolled her eyes again and changed the subject.

"What do you think all of our old high school classmates are up to now?" asked Ellie. "Maybe we should look them up and see if anyone wants to help us put together a class reunion. Doesn't that sound like a fun idea?"

"We can play our new *Mature Trivia Game*. The rules are simple. When someone starts talking and telling a story and can't remember a word, we simply offer up the word!" explained Ellie.

"Have you noticed when you are talking, words seem to elude you these days? Happens to the best of us, but we seem to understand the word needed to complete another's thought." Ellie laughed.

"It's always good to help a *Sista or Brother* out so they don't feel *so damn old*, and it keeps the conversation going with good humor and fun!"

"I bet most of them are dead!" snapped Edith. "Sounds like a waste of time to me. I have zero interest in getting together with a bunch of old folks and discussing our ailments."

"Our ships have sailed," continued Edith. "This younger generation puts all their personal crap on a thing called Instagram or Facebook. I hear you gotta ask if someone will be your friend. How pathetic is that? Will you be my friend?" said Edith in disgust.

"You also have to have a computer and freakin' know how to use it. I have no intention of learning how to use a computer. Technology is definitely not for me. Yep, our ships have sailed past that shit."

Wow! This seemed like a great time to bring up something important to Ellie's dear friend.

"What else have you been up to, Edith? Tell me about that short storybook your daughter Evelyn gave you to read. What's the name of it again?" asked Ellie.

"That weird book?" responded Edith.

"OOOH Crap! We Become What We Think About," roared Edith.

"Isn't that the dumbest name anyone's ever heard?"

"It says right here, **'Give yourself permission to start a new path.'** What the hell is that supposed to mean?"

"It's a little too late for me to be starting a new path at 77 years old!"

"It's called a **'StoryBookPath,'**" Edith said with sarcasm.

"And I certainly don't have time to hear about some ridiculous stories!"

"I'm no damn kid, that's for sure!"

Damn!...DAMN!!...and *shit fire, shit!!!*

Ellie and Evelyn had really hoped Edith would be open-minded and find the time to read the informative book and join the 30-day entry level path to personal development.

It seemed so perfect and such a simple way to help Edith so she wouldn't have an excuse for every opportunity presented in her life.

Ellie did her level best to carry on the conversation with her friend Edith, but she felt more disheartened and challenged with every topic.

"How have you been feeling, Edith?" Ellie asked, being truly concerned about her long-time friend.

"Well, my days are filled with aches and pains. My back hurts all the time, so I take Aleve twice a day. It helps me with my morning headaches too. You haven't lived until you can get through a day with this old body. Growing old ain't for sissies!!"

"Dr. Quack says I need more self-care. What the fuck does he know about me?" quipped Edith.

"For what it's worth, I think your doctor is correct. More self-care never hurt anyone," offered Ellie, with love and compassion. "You can start with nutritious meals. I have plenty of good, yummy recipes I can share."

"Quack, Quack, Quack!!!!" replied Edith.

"Don't tell me you're siding with that nut job, Quack!"

"Do you think you are struggling with grief? It's perfectly normal to feel aches and pains after you lose someone you love, especially if you haven't totally processed the grief," said Ellie as gently as possible. Ellie had thought long and hard about bringing this up, and she'd decided to ask Edith the question.

"Gotta go, my dryer is buzzing. Talk to you next week. Bye now, love ya!" And just like that, Edith hung up her phone and shut down THAT conversation.

As if on autopilot, Edith carried on with her limiting beliefs and excuses while Ellie tolerated their weekly phone conversations. She'd made the decision to love her friend even though her excuses were almost unbearable.

Edith's form of excuse-making is withdrawal, or disengagement. The excuses are made to continue participating in actions that are unhealthy, painful, and unsafe. However, we can find building blocks to a life of hope and a better future. By making the most of yourself, you make the world a better place to live.

Give yourself permission to take a new path. All you need is the plan, the road map, and the courage to move forward.

Join the 30-Day,
Entry Level program for Personal Development.

We provide heartfelt, entertaining, real-life stories of adversity about the challenges of overcoming the after-effects endured from psychological and emotional childhood/young adult trauma.

Free Introductory Guidebook, '*OOOH Crap!*
WE BECOME WHAT WE THINK ABOUT'
when you sign up at
WWW.STORYBOOKPATH.COM.

Meet the Authors

Janet Snyder, is the creator of *StoryBookPath.com a 30-day personal development program* and eBook designed to help you discover and live the life you love and desire. After finding her enthusiastic, authentic voice and true strength from her own personal struggle with the negative aftereffects endured from mental and emotional childhood/young adult trauma, Janet's fulfilling her life purpose of helping others.

Also, Founder of *StoryBook Cottages*, she uses her well-earned degree for interior design and her vivacious love of the earth designing playhouses constructed from recycled materials and sustainable living green rooftops. Janet is the mother of three and a "Nan" to her grandchildren who also live in her hometown of Louisville, Kentucky.

Kathleen Canova, successful entrepreneur and founder of the Canova Group, LLC, has facilitated and educated many regarding domestic crisis intervention, including deep emotional and spiritual healing practices. Rooted from her own lived experiences, and after extensive training and certifications, she shares her heartfelt hope, passion and inspiration with humankind.

Living in Westminster, Colorado near her adult children and grandchildren, who affectionately call her "Yaya," she enjoys spending quality time with family and friends when she's not reading, writing and traveling.

Sales Page

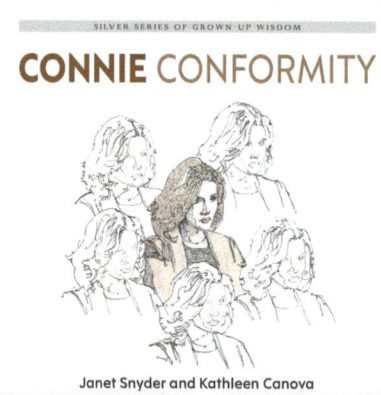

First-Time Co-Authors:

Janet Snyder and Kathleen Canova

Available on Amazon and Ingram-Spark now

www.storybookpath.com

On FACEBOOK: STORYBOOKPATH & SILVER SISTERS WISDOM

janet@storybookpath.com & kathleenkarrercanova@gmail.com